What they don't tell about

TILES & STONES

What they don't tell about

TILES & STONES

Abhishek Malani

Available on amazonkindle

Worldwide Published by

Pendown Press

PREMIUM BUSINESS PUBLISHER

PENDOWN PRESS LLP

An ISO 9001 & ISO 14001 Certified Co.,

Regd. Office: 3767A, Kanhaiya Nagar,

Tri Nagar, Delhi-110035

Ph.: 8130886000, 9650072927, 8595249536

E-mail: info@pendownpress.com

Branch Office: 1A/2A, 20, Hari Sadan, Ansari Road,

Daryaganj, New Delhi-110002

Ph.: 011-45794768

Website: PendownPress.com

Edition: 2025

Price: ₹ 399

ISBN: 978-81-989619-7-6

Layout and Cover Designed by Pendown Graphics Team

Printed and Bound in India by Thomson Press India Ltd.

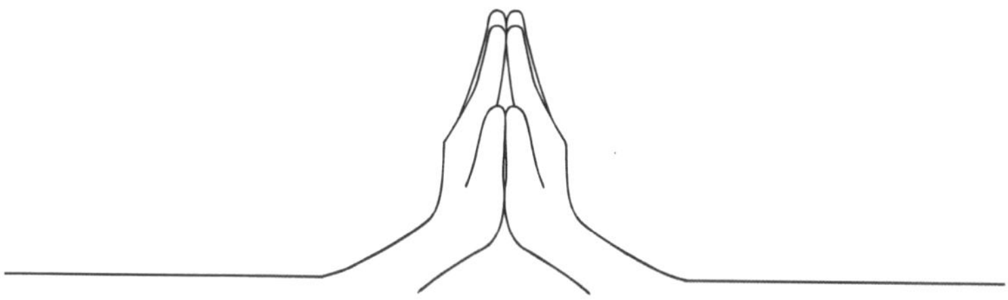

Dedication

To all the dreamers who turn empty spaces into meaningful homes—with love, vision, and care.

Table of Contents

Part 3: From Showroom to Site: How to Avoid Regret

Part 4: From Showroom to Site: How to Avoid Regret

Preface

First of all, thank you for picking up this book. Whether you're building your dream home, renovating a space, or simply curious to learn—you're in the right place.

After spending years in this industry, I've met all kinds of people: homeowners confused by too many choices, architects looking for reliable materials, contractors stuck between timelines and expectations, and shopkeepers trying to explain finishes and rates without losing patience.

One thing I've realised is that everyone wants to make the right decision—they just don't always get the right guidance. Some fall into traps of bad advice, some rush into purchases, and some simply don't know what questions to ask.

That's why I wrote this book.

Not as an expert preaching from above, but as someone who has stood on dusty sites, helped choose the right tiles, solved real-life laying problems, and seen the joy on people's faces when it all comes together just right.

This book doesn't use big words. It doesn't assume you know technical terms. It speaks to you the way I would if we were sitting across from each other, having a chai and discussing your flooring plans.

If this book helps even one person make a better, smarter, and stress-free choice—it will have done its job.

– Abhishek Malani

Acknowledgements

This book would not have been possible without the support of many people who have been part of my journey.

Whatever I have achieved in life is deeply rooted in the blessings of my grandparents and the unwavering support of my parents, both my uncles (Kakas), aunt (Bua), and sisters. Their presence in my life, especially my uncles and aunt, has been a constant source of strength, guidance, and unconditional love. I'm sincerely thankful for the role they've played in my journey.

To all my teachers, business coaches, and mentors who taught me and helped me reach this stage — thank you.

To my clients—thank you for trusting me with your homes, ideas, and challenges. Every project has been a learning opportunity.

To my suppliers and collaborators across the years—your integrity and partnership have helped me grow and serve better.

To my AVM Granite team—your commitment, resilience, and day-to-day efforts form the backbone of everything we do.

To my family - Veena, Bhaskar and Mukund - thank you for your patience, encouragement, and belief in my vision.

To my friends who have always been there for my support.

And finally, to every Architect, Civil Engineer, Contractor, Tile Installer and Homeowner who strives to build responsibly and beautifully—you are the reason this book exists.

A special acknowledgement goes to Dinesh Verma and his exceptional team at Pendown Press. From the initial concept to the final manuscript, their support and expertise have made this book possible.

Without the support of all of you, it would not have been possible for me to move forward with confidence.

Know Your Author

Abhishek Malani is a seasoned entrepreneur and the founder of **AVM Granite,** a company widely recognized for its excellence in the field of granite, tiles, and natural surface materials. With over 28 years of rich and hands-on experience, Abhishek has earned a solid reputation for quality, integrity, and deep industry knowledge in the architectural surface solutions space.

From humble beginnings to leading a ₹25 crore enterprise, his journey is a testament to relentless hard work, innovation, and an unwavering commitment to customer satisfaction. Over the years, he has personally guided thousands of homeowners, architects, and builders in choosing the right flooring and wall materials—expertly balancing aesthetics with performance.

Abhishek is widely respected not just for his technical knowledge, but also for his ability to break down complex decisions into simple, practical advice. His passion for educating clients led to the creation of this book—an effort to demystify the world of surface materials for new home builders, professionals, and design enthusiasts.

When he isn't working onsite or consulting clients, Abhishek spends his time exploring emerging design trends, mentoring young professionals, and championing ethical business practices within the construction and interiors industry.

He lives in Hubli, India, with his family and continues to drive innovation and trust through every tile and slab delivered by AVM Granite.

Why I Wrote This Book

After nearly three decades in the business of granite, tiles, and natural stones, I've had the privilege of working with thousands of home builders, architects, interior designers, and contractors. Across all these experiences, one common thread I've observed is the sheer confusion and lack of structured information when it comes to choosing the right flooring and wall cladding materials.

Every home is a dream, and every square foot laid is a long-term commitment —both emotional and financial. Yet, I've seen countless clients either overwhelmed by the endless choices or misled by trends, often settling for solutions that fail to align with their lifestyle, budget, or climate conditions. In many cases, poor decisions lead to regret, rework, or even long-term dissatisfaction. This book is my effort to bridge that gap.

Whether you're a homeowner building from scratch, an architect refining a design, or a builder looking to guide clients better—this guide is for you. **My goal is simple:** to help you choose materials not just by look, but by logic.

Who This Book Is For

- **New Home Builders:** If you're navigating flooring options for the first time, this book offers a clear, jargon free guide.
- **Architects & Interior Designers:** Use this as a practical reference for material selection, specifications, and balancing design with long-term performance.
- **Civil Contractors & Site Engineers:** A helpful companion to ensure flawless execution based on correct installation principles.
- **Students of Architecture and Design:** A compact yet comprehensive understanding of the Indian flooring industry.

Who This Book Is For

Words of Praise

Building a home is both a creative pursuit and a lifelong investment—every choice matters, especially when it comes to the surfaces we live with every day. This book is an outstanding companion for anyone involved in that journey. With clarity and authority, it illuminates the art and science of selecting tiles, wall claddings, and natural stones to help readers make informed and confident choices.

I have been consistently impressed by the quality, variety, and service offered at AVM Granite, Hubballi. Their extensive collection of tiles and natural stones caters to both contemporary and traditional architectural styles, making them a preferred destination for builders and institutions alike.

This insightful book, brought out by Mr. Abhishek Malani of AVM Granite, is a valuable resource for home builders, offering clear guidance on choosing the right tiles, wall claddings, and stones.

Dr. Ashok Shettar
Pro-Chancellor, KLE Technological University
Hubballi

What You'll Learn

- This book isn't just about products—it's about practical, real-world decision-making that leads to better results and lasting satisfaction
- The differences between Granite, Marble, Tiles and various other options —so you can choose what truly fits your space, budget, and lifestyle
- Which finishes work best in specific areas like kitchens, bathrooms, exteriors, and living spaces—and why
- How to select materials based on functionality, aesthetics, and longevity
- The importance of adhesives, spacers, grouts, and aftercare
- How to avoid costly mistakes and execute like a pro

My Philosophy

Good flooring isn't about what's trending. It's about what truly fits your lifestyle, your space, and your future needs. A well-chosen surface doesn't just elevate the beauty of a room—it improves functionality, comfort, and value.

This book is written from experience—grounded, site tested, and customer backed.

Thank you for allowing me to be a part of your homebuilding journey. It's an honor to help you make one of the most meaningful and lasting decisions for your living space.

Abhishek Malani

Founder, AVM Granite

Part 1

The Tile Truths No One Tells You

Introduction

Why Choosing the Right Tile is a Big Deal

Tiles may seem like a small part of construction, but in reality, they hold a lot more weight both literally and emotionally. They're what your feet touch every day, what your guests notice when they enter, and what your home silently carries, year after year.

And yet, time and again, I've seen people take tile decisions lightly.

Have you ever stepped into a freshly done home and noticed slippery surfaces, cracked edges, or tiles that just don't feel right underfoot? Or maybe you've experienced discoloration, swelling, or water seepage just a few months after laying them? These aren't rare occurrences. They're common, frustrating, and expensive to fix.

Here's the truth: it's not always the fault of the tile. Most of the time, it's because the tile was **wrongly selected for the space**.

Choosing tiles isn't just about matching colors with your wall paint or choosing the trendiest finish. It's about the **purpose**, the **footfall**, the **weather**, the **usage pattern**, and even your **lifestyle habits**. A gorgeous tile can turn into a nightmare if it's slippery in a bathroom or too soft for an outdoor parking area.

Over the years, I've worked with homeowners, architects, contractors, and even interior designers. Many of whom regret their early flooring choices. Not because they lacked taste, but because they weren't told what to ask, check, or understand.

This book exists to save you from that regret.

It will help you pause and ask questions that actually matter: **Where are you using this tile? What will it face? Can it handle moisture, weight, heat, cleaning?**

Because once tiles are installed, they're not easy to replace and mistakes here can haunt you every single day.

So don't just choose what looks good. Tiles aren't just a part of your home. They're part of your daily life. Choose wisely.

Tiles vs. Natural Stone vs. Modern Alternatives

What Really Works for You?

When it comes to flooring and wall surfaces, one of the most confusing decisions is choosing between tiles, natural stone, or modern alternatives like engineered quartz, SPC, or composite marble. Each option has its strengths and potential drawbacks, depending on where and how it's used.

Tiles are durable, cost-effective, and come in countless designs. From wood-look planks to stone-finish slabs, they're easy to clean and install. However, low-grade tiles can be slippery, chip over time, or lose their shine if not laid and maintained properly.

Natural stones like marble, granite, kota, and sandstone offer timeless charm. Each piece is unique, and their earthy tones suit both traditional and modern homes. But stones are porous and require sealing, skilled laying, and periodic maintenance to keep them looking good.

Modern alternatives such as **SPC flooring**, **composite marble**, and **sintered stone** are designed for high performance. They're resistant to stains, scratches, and moisture—making them ideal for kitchens, bathrooms, and renovation projects. They're also lighter and often quicker to install.

What works best for you?

- Want **low maintenance and affordability?** Go for vitrified tiles with anti-skid or matte finishes.
- Prefer **natural beauty and richness?** Choose natural stones but be ready for sealing and gentle upkeep.
- Working on a **tight timeline or rented space?** Laminate flooring or sheet vinyl might be your best bet.
- Looking for **luxury with uniformity?** Engineered quartz, composite marble, sintered stones, or large-format vitrified slabs deliver it with less fuss."
- Need **eco-conscious options?** Opt for recycled or responsibly sourced materials–available in both tiles and modern surfaces.

In short, the best choice is the one that fits your **space, usage, lifestyle, and long-term expectations**.

What's Next?

Now that you have a basic understanding of the main surface options, this book dives deeper into each category–from ceramic tiles to limestone, from wooden floors to SPC and engineered materials.

You'll discover real-world pros and cons, laying methods, maintenance tips, and practical buying advice–all tailored to Indian conditions and everyday budgets.

So, if you're still wondering which floor or wall surface is truly right for you, keep reading. The answers are just a few pages away.

Part 2
Choose With Confidence

CHAPTER 1

Granite

The Foundation of Indian Flooring

Granite is one of the most revered materials in architecture, known for its strength, elegance, and longevity. Formed through the slow crystallization of magma beneath the Earth's surface, granite is composed primarily of quartz, feldspar, and mica—resulting in a stone that is exceptionally hard, dense, and visually stunning. Its continued presence in Indian homes and commercial buildings for decades speaks volumes of its functional value and timeless appeal.

As someone who has worked with granite for over 28 years, I've seen its incredible adaptability—from luxurious bungalows and high traffic airports to kitchen countertops and serene pooja rooms. Its ability to blend tradition with modernity makes it a material of choice across generations and design styles. This chapter aims to guide you through understanding, selecting, and using granite effectively.

Varieties of Granite

India is one of the largest granite-producing countries in the world, offering a rich palette of colours, patterns and grains. It also imports some of the finest granites from across the world.

Just to mention a few of the most popular varieties — these can be grouped based on region, aesthetics and technical properties:

South Indian Granites

- **Black Galaxy (Andhra Pradesh)**: Jet black with golden specks; perfect for kitchens, staircases, and retail counters.
- **Absolute Black (Telangana)**: Deep solid black; favored for sleek interiors, tabletops, and monuments.
- **Steel Grey (Andhra Pradesh)**: A medium grey tone that fits well in both formal and casual spaces.
- **Tan Brown (Telangana):** Earthy brown with black flecks; excellent for warm-toned interiors and traditional aesthetics.
- **Vizag Blue**: Shades of blue and grey; ideal for temples, façades, and traditional cladding.
- **Kuppam Green**: Pale green with fine grain; suitable for garden pathways, outdoor flooring, and patios.
- **Sira Grey:** Coarse-grained grey granite, widely used in commercial and industrial spaces due to its strength and economy.

North Indian Granites

- **Jhansi Red (Uttar Pradesh)**: Vibrant red with dark crystals; commonly used in outdoor and heritage projects.
- **Rosy Pink (Rajasthan)**: Soft pink and grey tones; budget friendly and popular in mass housing.

- **Platinum White/Crystal Yellow**: Light tones with consistent patterns; often used in clean, minimalist designs.
- **Lakha Red**: Bold red stone with crystalline texture; preferred for temple flooring and exterior walls.

Exotic & Imported Granites

- **Blue Pearl (Norway):** Metallic shimmer with bold character; a true showstopper in premium spaces.
- **Titanium Gold (Brazil)**: Black base with swirling gold; used in luxury kitchens.
- **Emerald Pearl (Norway)**: Deep green with silver crystals; ideal for striking countertops and accent walls.
- **Cafe Brown (Brazil):** Rich chocolate tone with darker veining; adds warmth to interiors and worktops.

Granite Finishes and Their Applications

Granite finishes significantly affect both aesthetics and performance. Choosing the right finish not only enhances the visual appeal but also determines how the surface behaves in different conditions.

- **Polished Finish**
    - Glossy, reflective surface
    - **Ideal for:** Living rooms, dining halls, kitchen countertops, reception desks.
    - **Applications:** Enhances brightness in low-light interiors; used where elegance is key.
    - **Pros:** Enhances color, easy to clean, luxurious look.
    - **Cons:** Slippery when wet.

- **Honed Finish**
  - Smooth but matte surface
  - **Ideal for:** Bathrooms, corridors, soft modern interiors.
  - **Applications:** Preferred in areas that require subtle sophistication without glare.
  - **Pros:** Slip-resistant, subtle appeal.
  - **Cons:** Needs sealing more often.
- **Flamed Finish**
  - Rough, textured finish created by heat
  - **Ideal for:** Outdoor paving, pool decks, entry steps.
  - **Applications:** Offers excellent traction in wet or high-traffic external spaces.
  - **Pros:** Anti-skid and weatherproof.
  - **Cons:** Coarse underfoot.
- **Leathered Finish**
  - Textured with a soft sheen
  - **Ideal for:** Kitchen islands, bar counters, feature walls.
  - **Applications:** Popular in luxury kitchens for its tactile, fingerprint resistant quality.
  - **Pros:** Hides smudges, unique feel.
  - **Cons:** Slightly harder to clean.
- **Bush Hammered Finish**
  - Heavily textured, nonslip surface
  - **Ideal for:** Public areas, garden paths, water features.
  - **Applications:** Effective in spaces where maximum grip is needed, such as ramps and driveways.
  - **Pros:** Excellent grip.

- **Cons:** Difficult to maintain indoors.

➢ **Sandblasted Finish**

- Evenly textured using sand pressure
- **Ideal for:** Façades, decorative walls, swimming pool surrounds.
- **Applications:** Adds a uniform texture while maintaining slip resistance.
- **Pros:** Uniform finish, slip resistant.
- **Cons:** Can accumulate dirt.

Applications of Granite

➢ Granite is a truly **versatile material**. Here's where you can confidently use it:

- Flooring in residences, hotels, and offices
- Kitchen countertops and islands
- Staircases and landings
- Bathroom vanities and ledges
- Cladding for exteriors and boundary walls
- Landscaping: pavers, benches, garden steps
- Temple floors and steps
- Shopping mall entrances and corridor skirtings

➢ **Durability and Performance**

- **Lifespan:** 40–50 years with minimal wear
- **Strength:** High compressive strength and scratch resistance
- **Heat Resistance:** Excellent for hot cookware and Indian summers

- **Porosity:** Lower in darker granites; light-coloured stones need sealing

➢ Pros and Cons

- **Advantages**
  - Timeless appearance
  - Low maintenance (especially dark varieties)
  - High resale value
  - Natural and eco-friendly
  - Suitable for all climates
- **Disadvantages**
  - Feels hard and cold underfoot
  - Heavy (requires sturdy RCC base)
  - Limited flexibility in color matching
  - Can be expensive depending on finish and rarity

Buying Guide

1. Inspect full slabs under natural light for **color and vein uniformity**.
2. **Check thickness:** 18–20mm is standard for flooring; 20–30mm for countertops.
3. **Look for surface finish quality:** Avoid microcracks, resin patches, or uneven polish.
4. **Choose consistent batches:** Always source from the same lot for uniform shade.
5. **Confirm origin and warranty:** Reputed quarries offer better consistency and after-sales support.
6. **Discuss sealing and maintenance:** Especially important for lighter granites or polished surfaces.

7. **Ask for sample installation photos:** This helps visualize the stone in real-world environments.
8. **Ensure compatible adhesive grades**:
    - For standard indoor applications, use **C1T** or **C2T** grade adhesives.
    - For heavy-duty or wet areas like exterior cladding, wet balconies, or bathroom walls, opt for **C2TES1** or **C2TES2** class adhesives as per EN 12004.

Installation Guide

1. **Surface Preparation**: Ensure the base is flat, clean, and free of debris.
2. **Dry Laying**: Arrange slabs on site before fixing to ensure grain flow and aesthetic pattern.
3. **Apply Bonding Agent**: Use a suitable granite adhesive:
    a. **C1T/C2T** for dry internal flooring,
    b. **C2TES1** for kitchens, washrooms, and high-traffic indoor areas,
    c. **C2TES2** for external cladding and wet environments.
4. **Set Slabs Carefully** – Align with a rubber mallet and check levels with a spirit level.
5. **Joint Filling** – Use non-shrinking, stain free epoxy grout or color-matched filler.
6. **Edge Finishing** – Polish edges or apply the desired finish for skirting and thresholds.
7. **Curing and Cleaning** – Allow 24–48 hours for setting before sealing or heavy use. Use pH neutral cleaners for long-term maintenance.

Tip: Always engage skilled professionals with experience in natural stone installation, especially for high-end finishes or large format slabs.

Final Thoughts

Granite has long held its place as a **symbol of natural strength and enduring elegance**, especially in high-traffic and premium construction projects. With the right selection and expert installation, it continues to perform reliably in commercial and institutional settings, delivering unmatched durability.

However, its use in residential flooring has significantly declined in recent years. The limited availability of lighter-toned granites—often preferred in modern home interiors—along with the growing scarcity of high-quality reserves, has made granite a less viable choice for everyday homes. Issues such as discoloration and rust formation after installation, excessive pigmentation by some manufacturers, and rising material and transportation costs have further reduced its appeal among homeowners.

Today's market offers better-performing alternatives like vitrified tiles and engineered stones that are not only cost-effective but also offer greater design flexibility and consistency.

That said, granite still holds significant value in select applications. Certain varieties are well-suited for landscaping, Window sills, Door frames, and Exterior Wall cladding - where their strength and weather resistance shine. Exotic granites, with their striking patterns and rich colours, also make excellent choices for feature walls or accent surfaces or Counter Tops - lending a sense of grandeur when used thoughtfully.

While its era as a mainstream flooring solution may be drawing to a close, granite remains a noble material—one that is best reserved today for specialized roles that celebrate its true strengths and natural character.

CHAPTER 2

Indian Marble

Timeless Elegance Rooted in Indian Tradition

Indian marble has long been revered for its natural beauty, cultural significance, and accessibility. With a legacy woven into temples, palaces, and monuments like the Taj Mahal, Indian marble stands as a symbol of grace and sophistication. Thanks to its wide availability, cost-effectiveness, and compatibility with the Indian climate, it remains one of the most popular choices for flooring and wall cladding across the country.

With nearly three decades of experience in the stone industry, I've had the opportunity to work with all major types of Indian marble. This chapter offers practical insights into choosing, applying, and maintaining Indian marble for a variety of residential and commercial projects.

A Few Popular Varieties of Indian Marble

➢ **White and Off-White Marbles:**

- **Makrana White**: Pristine, dense, and historically significant. Used in temples and luxury residences.
- **Dungri and Albeta (Makrana region)**: Soft white with light veining; more affordable than Makrana White.

- **Morwad White**: Slightly grey toned white; commonly used in North India.
- **Ambaji White**: Subtle white marble with minimal veining.

➢ **Colored and Decorative Marbles:**

- **Katni Marble**: Cream, beige, and light green tones; great for warm interior themes.
- **Banswara Marble (White and Purple)**: Unique violet and white mix, adds a vibrant yet traditional feel.
- **Green Marble (Udaipur)**: Deep green with white veins; striking in contrast-rich designs.
- **Pink Marble (Udaipur)**: Warm pink tones; often used in heritage or classical architecture.

Available Finishes

➢ **Polished**: Glossy surface that enhances color and grain; widely used in living spaces.

➢ **Honed**: Matte finish offering an elegant, non-reflective look; suitable for large floors and bathrooms.

➢ **Antique/Tumbled**: Weathered texture for rustic, vintage vibes.

➢ **Sandblasted**: Lightly textured finish for exterior walls and patios.

Applications of Indian Marble

➢ Living and dining room flooring

➢ Bathroom walls and countertops

➢ Staircases and lobby areas

- Traditional pooja rooms and temple floors
- Columns, skirting, and wall cladding
- Inlay work for borders and medallions

Indian marble is often used in combination with other stones like granite or sandstone to create elaborate patterns and thematic zones.

Performance and Maintenance

- **Durability:** 20–30 years with routine maintenance
- **Scratch Resistance:** Moderate; avoid dragging heavy furniture
- **Water Absorption:** Higher than granite; needs regular sealing
- **Stain Sensitivity:** Prone to etching from acids like lemon, vinegar

Pros and Cons

Advantages:

- Naturally elegant and luminous
- Easily available across India
- Affordable compared to imported marble
- Can be repolished multiple times
- Compatible with both heritage and modern design themes

Disadvantages

- Softer and more porous than granite
- Requires sealing and maintenance
- Susceptible to stains and scratches

Buying Guide

When purchasing Indian marble, take the following practical steps to ensure you get the best **value and quality**:

1. **Inspect Full Slabs in Daylight:** Natural light reveals the true color, veining, and any surface imperfections like hairline cracks or fill marks.
2. **Check for Uniformity:** Make sure the shade, thickness, and texture are consistent across all slabs. Irregularities can lead to visible mismatches post-installation.
3. **Select from the Same Quarry Batch:** Always request marble slabs from the same lot or batch to minimize variation in tone and grain.
4. **Assess Water Absorption and Porosity:** Higher porosity increases maintenance. Ask your supplier for technical data or conduct a water-drop test.
5. **Ask About Polishing:** Factory polished slabs tend to be more uniform and easier to install. Site polished options may be required for seamless joints but depend on skilled labour. However, for a seamless look and feel of the marble, it needs to be polished on-site post laying.
6. **Decide on Finish Type in Advance:** The choice of finish (polished, honed, tumbled) should suit both the application and expected maintenance routine.
7. **Verify Thickness and Edge Quality:** Flooring slabs are usually 16–18 mm. For counters and vanity tops, go for 20–25 mm. Smooth, machine cut edges reduce laying issues.
8. **Inquire About Sealing and Pretreatment**: Especially important for light-coloured marble, which is more stain prone.

9. **Choose a Trusted Supplier:** Work with reputed vendors who offer quality assurance, proper packing, and support in case of post-installation issues.

Installation Guide

Proper installation is crucial to the long-term performance and beauty of Indian marble. Here's a detailed step-by-step guide:

1. **Substrate Preparation**
    a. Clean and level the surface.
    b. Ensure there is no loose debris or moisture before laying.
    c. Use a slope where water drainage is necessary (e.g., balconies, washrooms).
2. **Marble Conditioning**
    a. Soak slabs in clean water for at least 1–2 hours before installation. This pre-wetting process reduces the marble's tendency to absorb moisture from the adhesive or mortar, which can otherwise lead to uneven curing, discoloration, and patchy surfaces. It also helps in achieving a more consistent bond and finish, especially for light-coloured or highly porous varieties of marble.
    b. In some cases of Pure White Marble or Very Light Shade Marbles, a Coating of White Cement Slurry should be applied on the rear surface of the slab to avoid mortar absorption.
3. **Adhesive and Mortar Selection**
    a. **For most internal dry areas:** White cement slurry or C1T tile adhesive.

b. **For kitchens, bathrooms, or damp prone zones:** C2TE or C2TES1 grade adhesives.

c. **For exterior wall cladding or wet zones:** C2TES2 class adhesive is highly recommended.

d. Use White Colour Adhesives

4. **Laying Technique**

    a. Apply the adhesive using a notched trowel for consistent spread.

    b. Align slabs carefully using spacers and rubber mallets.

    c. For vein matched layouts, dry lay the design beforehand to ensure visual flow.

5. **Jointing and Levelling**

    a. Keep joints minimal (1–2 mm) for a seamless look.

    b. Fill joints with white cement and marble powder mix, or use epoxy grout in a matching shade.

6. **Polishing**

    a. Allow proper curing (at least 3–4 days) before starting machine polishing.

    b. Start with coarse grit and gradually move to finer ones for a mirror-like finish.

    c. For better results and stain resistance, use pre-polishing deep-penetrating sealers.

7. **Sealing**

    a. Apply a penetrating marble sealer, especially for light shades and bathroom use.

    b. Reseal every 1–2 years, depending on usage and exposure.

8. **Cleaning & Maintenance**
   a. Avoid acid-based cleaners which can etch and damage the marble surface.
   b. Use pH neutral, marble-safe cleaning solutions with a soft mop.

Tip: Use felt pads under furniture legs and avoid dragging metal objects to prevent scratches on the marble surface.

Final Thoughts

Indian marble has traditionally offered a beautiful balance of affordability, natural elegance, and deep cultural significance. For decades, it has adorned homes—from those rooted in classical tradition to modern villas seeking a connection to nature—offering timeless charm and versatile application.

However, in recent years, Indian marble has seen a decline in preference, particularly in premium residences. The growing dominance of imported marbles, known for their consistent textures, lighter tones, and refined finishes, has gradually shifted the market landscape. Moreover, some of India's most iconic varieties—such as Makrana and Ambaji—have become increasingly scarce and prohibitively expensive due to limited quarrying and over extraction. These heritage stones now see more limited use, often reserved for places of worship, restoration work, or highly curated spaces.

Despite this shift, Indian marble still holds significant value in contexts where authenticity, tradition, and warmth are priorities. When sourced wisely, installed properly, and maintained with care, it continues to lend grace and individuality to the spaces it inhabits. Whether as a statement staircase, a traditional pooja room floor, or elegant inlay work—its presence can evoke both nostalgia and pride.

Yet, its widespread popularity has clearly made way for more globally sourced materials that better meet the evolving demands of today's high-end architectural aesthetics.

CHAPTER 3

Imported Marble

Global Luxury in Indian Living

Imported marble brings unmatched refinement, consistency, and sophistication to interior design. Sourced from countries like Italy, Spain, Greece, Turkey, and Vietnam, these marbles are prized for their high purity, exquisite veining, and larger format slabs that minimize joint lines and create a seamless look. Often pre-polished and resin-treated at the source, they are perfect for luxury homes, boutique hotels, and premium commercial spaces seeking elegance with minimal maintenance.

Having worked with premium imported marble for over two decades, I can confidently say it transforms not just spaces—but experiences. Its presence instantly elevates the ambience, making it a preferred choice for discerning clients. This chapter helps you understand its selection, application, installation, and long-term care.

A Few Popular Types of Imported Marble

- **Statuario (Italy)**: Iconic white marble with bold grey veining; perfect for statement interiors.
- **Carrara (Italy)**: Subtle grey veins on a white base; elegant and timeless.

- **Calacatta (Italy)**: Dramatic, thick veining with high contrast; luxurious and bold.
- **Crema Marfil (Spain)**: Creamy beige base; warm, classic, and versatile.
- **Grey William (Italy/Greece/Turkey)**: Earthy greys with linear patterns; suits contemporary themes.
- **Vietnam White**: Consistent bright white; ideal for minimal and modern interiors.
- **Dyna (Italy/Turkey)**: Beige marble with wavy textures; well-liked in upscale Indian homes.

Available Finishes

- **Polished**: Most common, mirror-like surface
- **Honed**: Smooth, matte finish for muted elegance and low glare
- **Antiqued / Leathered**: Textured finish that offers a natural, vintage feel
- **Book Matched**: Carefully arranged slabs with mirrored veins for dramatic walls and floors

Applications

- Living room floors and foyers
- Feature walls and double-height lobbies
- Bathroom countertops and dry vanity areas
- Hotel reception desks and luxury retail spaces
- Staircases, lift lobbies, and boutique hallways

Note: Imported marble is rarely used in kitchens or exterior applications due to its high porosity and stain sensitivity. However, some varieties of Marbles like Travertine are used in the outdoor façades and landscaping when properly treated.

Performance and Maintenance

- **Durability:** 15–25 years, depending on use and care
- **Water Absorption:** Higher than granite; seal both before and after installation
- **Scratch Resistance:** Low to moderate; not recommended for high-abrasion zones
- **Etching:** Highly sensitive to acids like lemon, vinegar, and wine —wipe spills immediately

Pros and Cons

Advantages:

- Unmatched beauty and consistency
- Available in large, seamless slabs
- Prestigious and luxurious appeal
- Enhances property value

Disadvantages:

- Expensive material and handling
- Requires skilled installation
- Sensitive to staining and etching
- Needs regular sealing and specific maintenance

Buying Guide

1. **Choose slabs in person or via HD video:** Visual selection ensures correct veining and batch match.
2. **Verify slab size and thickness**: Most imported slabs are 18–20 mm; check for uniform thickness.
3. **Check surface treatment**: Most come resin-filled and pre-polished; ask for polish quality.
4. **Confirm moisture sensitivity**: Ask the supplier about porosity levels and required sealing procedures.
5. **Ask about storage and transit handling:** Imported marble is fragile; ensure proper crating and protection during transport.
6. **Match slabs for continuity**: Especially critical in book-matched or vein-matched designs.
7. **Choose from trusted importers**: Ensure product authenticity, documentation, and after-sales support.

Installation Guide

1. **Surface Preparation**
    a. Ensure a completely level and moisture-free substrate.
    b. Use a waterproof base in wet zones.
2. **Adhesive Recommendation**
    a. **For internal dry floors and walls:** C2T or C2TE grade adhesive
    b. **For bathrooms, spas, or moist areas:** C2TES1 or C2TES2 adhesive
    c. Use **White-coloured Adhesives** as it may stain light-coloured marble

3. **Cutting and Handling**
    a. Use diamond blades or waterjet cutters to minimize chipping
    b. Handle slabs with care due to fragile edges
4. **Laying Technique**
    a. Back-butter both the surface and slab with adhesive
    b. Use a rubber mallet for levelling; maintain 2 mm joint
    c. Avoid metal spacers, as they can rust and stain the marble
5. **Grouting and Joint Filling**
    a. Use non-staining epoxy grout in matching colours
    b. Clean excess immediately to avoid residue or residue
6. **Curing and Polishing**
    a. Do not use **acid-based chemicals** for cleaning
    b. Follow a minimum 7-step polishing process
    c. For Better results, go for Diamond Polishing Abrasives
    d. Go for Nano-based Pre-polish Sealing and Chemical Treatments to enhance the gloss, finish, and stain resistance
    e. Allow 2–3 days before final buffing or light use
7. **Sealing and Chemical Treatments**
    a. Use penetrating sealers specifically formulated for imported marble
    b. Apply one coat before installation (optional) and another after final cleaning
    c. Reapply sealers every 1–2 years for lasting stain resistance

    For enhanced protection, consider nano sealers or

fluoropolymer-based treatments (Pre-polish as well as post-finishing)

8. **Sustainable Finishing and Protection**
   a. Choose low-VOC, eco-friendly sealers for health and sustainability
   b. Use microfiber cloths and pH neutral cleaners for daily maintenance
   c. Avoid wax-based or film-forming coatings that reduce breathability

Tip: Educate housekeeping staff on proper cleaning methods and materials to avoid accidental etching or dulling of the marble surface.

Final Thoughts

Imported marble undoubtedly brings a sense of grandeur and refinement that can elevate interior spaces to luxurious heights. When carefully selected, expertly laid, and well-maintained, it becomes a hallmark of opulence and timeless taste—a material that speaks of elegance at first glance.

However, it's important to weigh the practical considerations alongside the aesthetic appeal. Imported marbles come with a significantly higher initial cost, both in terms of material itself and the specialized craftsmanship required for proper installation. Beyond that, they require ongoing maintenance – including periodic sealing, re-polishing, and delicate care - to retain their original luster. In high-use or humid areas, this can lead to substantial long-term effort and expense.

As modern design trends shift toward practical luxury, large-format vitrified slabs have emerged as a smarter and more sustainable alternative. Offering the visual elegance of marble with superior durability and minimal upkeep, these slabs replicate the aesthetics of natural stone while being more resistant to stains, scratches, and wear. They are also easier to install and maintain, making them ideal for contemporary lifestyles.

While imported marble still holds value for select, statement areas, large-format vitrified slabs are fast becoming the preferred choice for those who seek high-end appeal without compromising on performance, convenience, or cost-efficiency.

CHAPTER 4

Ceramic and Vitrified Tiles

Modern Versatility in Surface Design

Tiles have revolutionized flooring and wall finishes in the modern construction industry. Among the wide range of tile options available, ceramic and vitrified tiles stand out as the most practical, scalable, and design-flexible solutions for residential, commercial, and institutional spaces in India. Their adaptability to Indian climatic conditions, ease of maintenance, affordability, and aesthetic range make them an indispensable part of today's interior and architectural design.

As someone who has seen the transformation of the tile industry first hand over the past 28 years, I can confidently say that the rise of vitrified tiles in particular has been one of the most important developments in Indian surface material trends. What once began as a functional alternative has now matured into a design-forward, performance-driven solution. In this chapter, I will offer a comprehensive overview of both ceramic and vitrified tiles—how they are made, where they are used, what types and finishes are available, and how to select and install them correctly for maximum durability and design impact.

Brief Overview of Tiles

Tiles are not just surface coverings—they are engineered products manufactured with precision and purpose. Their composition and manufacturing process significantly affect their performance, durability, and aesthetics, which is why understanding the different types is crucial to making an informed choice.

Types of Tiles (Ceramic, Porcelain, Vitrified)

1. **Ceramic Tiles**

   Manufactured using natural clay mixed with water and minerals. The clay is shaped, dried, and fired in kilns at high temperatures ranging from (1000–1250°C). A glaze may be applied before the final firing to achieve various finishes and colors.

   - Softer and more porous compared to vitrified tiles.
   - Available in glazed and unglazed varieties.
   - Commonly used for wall cladding, bathroom floors, and kitchen backsplashes in low-traffic areas.
   - Easier to cut and install, making them suitable for DIY or decorative applications.

2. **Vitrified Tiles**

   Vitrified tiles are composed of a refined mix of clay, silica, quartz, and feldspar, and are fired at very high temperatures (1200–1250°C) to achieve vitrification. The result is a dense, nonporous, water-resistant tile suitable for almost all surfaces.

Common Subtypes of Vitrified Tiles:

1. **Full Body:**
   - Uniform color and design throughout the tile's body
   - Highly durable and ideal for heavy traffic areas such as malls, airports, and industrial spaces
2. **Double Charged:**
   - Two layers of pigment fused on top
   - Offers superior strength and long-lasting performance; great for offices, lobbies, and hospitals
3. **Glazed Vitrified Tiles (GVT):**
   - A printed decorative layer covered with a protective glaze
   - Offers unlimited design flexibility, including wood, marble, and stone lookalikes
4. **Polished Glazed Vitrified Tiles (PGVT):**
   - A high-gloss version of GVT with a mirror-like finish
   - Commonly used in living rooms, showrooms, and other areas requiring a luxurious aesthetic
5. **Colour Body:**
   - Surface color closely matches the color of the tile body
   - Reduces visibility of chips and wear, making it perfect for busy interiors like commercial offices, shops, and restaurants
6. **Soluble Salt:**
   - Printed using a salt-based solution before firing
   - A more economical option, suited for basic residential flooring where intensive design or high polish is not a priority

3. **Porcelain Tiles**

   A refined version of vitrified tiles, porcelain tiles are made using finer clay and fired at the highest temperatures among all tile categories. This results in a highly compact and dense structure, with a water absorption rate of less than 0.5%, making them suitable for both indoor and outdoor applications. Known for their strength, stain resistance, and finish variety, porcelain tiles are often favored in luxury environments like hotel lobbies, showrooms, and upscale bathrooms, where both performance and elegance are critical.

Comparison of Ceramic, Porcelain, and Vitrified Tiles

Property	Ceramic Tiles	Porcelain Tiles	Vitrified Tiles
Material Composition	Clay, quartz, and feldspar; glazed surface	Refined clay, silica, and feldspar	Clay with silica, quartz, feldspar (vitrified body)
Water Absorption	5-10%	<0.5%	<0.1%
Durability	Moderate	Very high	Highest
Surface Finish	Glossy, matte, textured	Glossy, matte, satin, textured	Glossy, matte, satin, rustic
Scratch Resistance	Lower than vitrified	High	Very high

Slip Resistance	Higher in matte variants	Moderate to high (depends on surface)	Depends on surface treatment
Firing Temperature	800 - 1000°C	1200-1300°C	1100-1250°C
Recommended Applications	Walls, low-traffic floors, indoor use	High-traffic floors, commercial & outdoor	Indoor & outdoor floors, commercial spaces
Cost	Low	Medium to High	Medium to High
Ease of Cutting	Easy	Harder to cut than ceramic	Harder to cut than ceramic
Maintenance	Easy to clean	Low maintenance	Low maintenance
Porosity	High	Very low	Negligible
Gloss Options	Available in multiple options	Wide range	Available in multiple types (PGVT, GVT, DC)
Colour/Design Penetration	Only on top surface (glazed)	Full body or glazed options	Top layer or full body depending on type
Thickness Range	5-8 mm	8-12 mm	8-15 mm

Comparison of Vitrified Tile Types

Property	Soluble Salt	GVT (Glazed Vitrified Tile)	PGVT (Polished Glazed Vitrified Tile)	Color Body	Full Body	Double Charge
Tile Type	Soluble Salt	GVT	PGVT	Color Body	Full Body	Double Charge
Surface Design Method	Ink dissolved and absorbed into surface	Digital printing on glazed surface	Digital printing + polishing	Glazed with color-matched body	Color and pattern throughout tile	Two layers of pigment pressed during manufacturing
Design Penetration	Only on top layer	Only on top glazed layer	Only on top glazed layer	Top layer only, but body color matches	Through body	3–4 mm top design layer

Water Absorption	<0.1%	<0.1%	<0.1%	<0.1%	<0.1%	<0.1%
Durability	Moderate	High	High	Very High	Very High	Very High
Scratch Resistance	Moderate	Good	Good (may reduce slightly due to polish)	High	Very High	Very High
Applications	Low-traffic areas, budget-friendly projects	Residential & light commercial use	Homes, showrooms, indoor use	High-traffic commercial areas	Airports, malls, industrial floors	High-traffic commercial & industrial areas
Cost	Low	Medium	Medium	High	High	Medium to High
Stain Resistance	Moderate	High	Moderate to high	High	Very High	High

UV Resistance	Low	Medium	Low to Medium	High	Very High	High
Slip Resistance	Low	Medium to High (depends on texture)	Low to Medium (depending on polish)	Medium to High	High	Medium to High
Thickness Range	8-10 mm	8-15 mm	8-15 mm	8-15 mm	8-15 mm	8-10 mm

Available Finishes

Finishes

- **Glossy:** Highly reflective, smooth surface that enhances brightness; best suited for low-traffic areas and decorative walls.
- **Matte:** Non-reflective, slip-resistant, and subtle in appearance; perfect for kitchens, bathrooms, and outdoor use.
- **Satin / High Gloss:** Intermediate shine between glossy and matte; offers elegance with slight reflectivity for premium interiors.
- **Carving / Punch / 3D Textured:** Etched or embossed surfaces with tactile depth; perfect for feature walls, décor panels, and artistic spaces.
- **Sugar Finish:** Slightly grainy surface with crystal-like texture; offers soft luster and a unique tactile feel.
- **Metallic:** Reflective surface with embedded metallic particles; often used in modern, futuristic design schemes.
- **GHR (Glazed High Resistance):** A durable, glossy finish designed for high-footfall zones; combines gloss with durability.
- **R10 / R11 Anti-Slip Ratings:** Standardized slip-resistance for wet areas. R10 provides grip (ideal for residential wet areas), while R11 is suitable for commercial kitchens, balconies, and exterior ramps.

Available Sizes

- **Standard Wall Tiles:** 300x600 mm, 300x450 mm
- **Floor Tiles:** 600x600 mm, 800x800 mm, 600x1200 mm

- **Large Format:** 800x1600 mm, 1200x2400 mm, and up to 1600x3200 mm slabs
- **Special Shapes:** Chevron, hexagonal, planks, and mosaics formats

Larger formats are increasingly preferred for seamless, minimal-joint aesthetics, especially in luxury and modern projects.

Design Possibilities in Tiles

Modern digital printing and advanced glazing technology have opened up an incredible array of design options in tiles. These innovations cater to a variety of aesthetic preferences, from traditional to contemporary, making tiles one of the most versatile design materials:

- **Marble Replicas:** Faithfully imitate premium marbles like Statuario, Calacatta, and Onyx with high accuracy at a fraction of the cost.
- **Stone Look and Feel:** Capture the raw, organic textures of natural stones like slate, sandstone, and quartzite with impressive depth and realism.
- **Wooden Look Tiles:** Designed to mimic timber planks, ideal for those wanting the warmth of wood with the practicality of tiles.
- **Tropical and Botanical Prints:** Lush foliage and floral motifs that add a fresh, exotic vibe to indoor and outdoor areas.
- **Moroccan Patterns:** Intricate geometric motifs in vibrant colours inspired by Middle Eastern and Mediterranean design.

- **Exotic Stones Look:** Replicate rare and luxurious materials like malachite, jade, and semi-precious crystals—perfect for statement walls or high-impact surfaces.
- **Geometric Patterns:** Contemporary lines, shapes, and optical illusions that give tiles a dynamic, artistic edge.
- **Concrete and Cement Finish:** Offer a raw, industrial aesthetic—perfect for urban minimalism and loft-style interiors.
- **Pastel Shades:** Soft, muted colour palettes that bring calmness and sophistication to interiors. Perfect for Scandinavian, minimal, or vintage inspired spaces.

Whether your design preference is earthy, elegant, eclectic, or edgy—tiles can bring your vision to life with precision, creativity, and long-lasting durability.

General Usage and Applications

Tiles are used in virtually every built environment. Below are some common application categories along with recommended tile types and reasons for their suitability:

Application Area	Recommended Tile Type	Reason for Recommendation
Residential Spaces - Living Rooms, Bathrooms, Bedrooms, Kitchens	Soluble Salt/ Double Charge/ PGVT / GVT / Colour Body / Full Body	Modern aesthetics, wide design options, and durability

Office Spaces	Colour Body / GVT	Durable, uniform colour with aesthetic appeal
Retail Showrooms	Colour Body / GVT	Attractive, scratch-resistant, Matt finish
High Footfall Commercial Areas	Full Body / Colour Body	Highly durable, suitable for continuous foot traffic
Hospital / Clinic	Full Body / Colour Body	Hygienic, resistant to chemicals and frequent cleaning
School / College	Colour Body / Full Body	Wear-resistant and easy to maintain
Hotel Lobbies	GVT / PGVT / Colour Body/ Full Body	Luxurious appearance with robust surface
Parking Area - Residential	GVT / Full Body - 12 mm or 15 mm	Strong, non-slip, suitable; suitable for light vehicular traffic
Parking Area - Commercial	GVT / Full Body - 15 mm	High strength, non-slip surface; suitable for heavy vehicular movement
Staircases	Full Body / Colour Body	Safe, durable and edge-resistant
Industrial Flooring	Full Body (High abrasion resistant) - 12mm or 15 mm	Resistant to impact, chemicals, and abrasion

Tiles can also be effectively used in staircases, terraces, swimming pools (typically mosaic tiles), and even elevators.

Life and Durability

High quality vitrified tiles have an average lifespan of 15–20 years under regular use. Some full body tiles, used in industrial or commercial projects, can last up to 25 years or more.

Key Performance Attributes:

- High load-bearing strength
- Low water absorption
- Scratch resistance (especially in double charged tiles)
- UV and chemical resistance (in outdoor-grade tiles)
- Easy to clean and maintain

Note: Ceramic tiles are more delicate and should be used only in low-wear zones.

Advantages and Disadvantages

Advantages

- Vast range of colors, sizes, textures, and finishes
- Cost-effective and easily available
- Faster installation compared to natural stone
- Consistent quality and uniformity
- Resistant to moisture, stains, and chemicals
- Minimal maintenance

Disadvantages

- Can crack under extreme impact
- Joints require grouting and periodic cleaning
- Lower resale value compared to natural stone (in premium segments)
- Can feel cold and hard underfoot

Buying Guide

1. **Define the space**: Is it for a wall, floor, dry area, or wet zone?
2. **Check the tile rating** –

   PEI Rating (Porcelain Enamel Institute): Indicates the tile's ability to resist surface wear. PEI ratings range from 0 to 5:

   a. **PEI 0**: No foot traffic (only for walls)

   b. **PEI 1–2**: Light traffic (bathrooms, bedrooms)

   c. **PEI 3**: Moderate traffic (residential floors)

   d. **PEI 4**: Heavy traffic (kitchens, corridors)

   e. **PEI 5**: Extra heavy traffic (commercial and public spaces)
3. **R-value (Slip Resistance Rating)** – Denotes the anti-slip characteristics of tiles, particularly important for wet and sloped surfaces:

   a. **R9**: Minimal slip resistance (indoor dry areas)

   b. **R10**: Moderate slip resistance (kitchens, bathrooms)

   c. **R11**: High slip resistance (outdoors, wet zones)

   d. **R12–R13**: Specialized use in industrial or extremely wet areas

- **Inspect finish and size**: Match the tile's aesthetics with the space and scale of the room.
- **Choose grout wisely**: Epoxy grout is more durable and stain-resistant than cement-based grout.
- **Buy extra**: Always purchase **5–10% extra** tiles to account for cuts, breakage, and wastage.
- **Verify brand and warranty**: Choose reliable brands with ISI/EN certification.

Laying Procedure

Tile Laying with Back Buttering and Spacers

1. **Substrate Preparation**
   a. Ensure the surface is level, clean, and free of debris or grease.
   b. Use a self-levelling compound if needed to correct floor undulations.
   c. In wet areas, apply a waterproofing membrane before installation.
2. **Adhesive Selection by Application**
   a. **For wall and floor tiles below 600x600 mm in dry areas:** Use C1T or C2T adhesive.
   b. **For wet areas like bathrooms, kitchens, and balconies:** Use C2TE or C2TES1 adhesive for superior adhesion and flexibility.
   c. **For large-format tiles above 800 mm or external applications:** Use C2TES2 grade adhesive with higher bond strength and deformability.

   d. Always follow the adhesive manufacturer's instructions for mixing and open time.

3. **Applying Adhesive**
   a. Use a notched trowel to spread the adhesive uniformly across the surface.
   b. For large format tiles (600x1200 mm and above), use the **back buttering technique**—a method where adhesive is applied not only on the substrate but also on the back of the tile. This ensures 100% contact, improves adhesion, and prevents air gaps that could lead to cracking or hollowness underfoot. Back buttering is highly recommended for uneven surfaces or heavy-duty applications such as exterior facades and large open floors.

4. **Tile Laying and Alignment**
   a. Use tile spacers to maintain uniform grout lines and to allow for thermal expansion and contraction. Spacers improve aesthetics and prevent stress cracking.
   b. Press tiles firmly and level them using a rubber mallet.
   c. Check alignment frequently using a laser or chalk line.

5. **Grouting**
   a. Allow tiles to set for 24 hours before grouting.
   b. Use epoxy grout in moisture prone or high-traffic areas for better stain resistance and durability.
   c. Use masking tapes on the tile surface at the joints before applying grout.
   d. Clean off excess grout immediately to avoid haze or permanent stains.

6. Cleaning and Final Curing

   a. Clean tile surfaces with a damp sponge and pH neutral cleaner.

   b. Avoid acid-based cleaners, which can damage the tile glaze and grout.

Important Tips

- Avoid walking on freshly laid tiles for at least 24–48 hours.
- Protect laid surfaces during ongoing construction to prevent damage.
- Always match the adhesive and grout grade to the tile type, format, and application zone.
- Avoid tight joints to reduce stress cracking. Always use spacers.
- Restrict all foot traffic for a minimum of 48 hours post laying.

Final Thoughts

Ceramic and vitrified tiles have become the backbone of modern surface solutions—offering an unmatched blend of aesthetics, durability, and innovation. Among them, vitrified tiles have emerged as the most advanced, adaptable, and future-ready material in the world of architectural finishes. Their superior strength, near-zero porosity, and wide array of designs make them an ideal choice across the spectrum—from compact urban apartments to sprawling luxury villas.

As a tile professional and trusted supplier, I believe the difference lies in understanding both the technical aspects and the real-world requirements of every space. When you align these two, tiles become more than a finish—they become a long-term investment in the quality, comfort, and experience of a space.

Today, we have vitrified tile solutions for virtually every practical application - flooring, wall cladding, wet areas, high-load parking zones, landscaping, and even countertops and staircase risers. Their versatility is unmatched, enabling seamless design continuity across indoor and outdoor environments.

With continuous innovation in textures, sizes, and finishes—whether it's marble-look PGVTs, rugged full-body tiles for industrial use, or anti-skid options for wet zones - vitrified tiles are no longer just an alternative to natural materials; they represent the smarter, more sustainable evolution of surface design.

As customer preferences shift toward low-maintenance luxury and value-driven design, vitrified tiles will continue to lead the way - redefining how India builds, sustains and beautifies its living spaces.

CHAPTER 5

Limestone
Kota and Tandoor

Enduring Simplicity with Natural Charm

Limestone has long held a special place in Indian architecture due to its affordability, natural appearance, and cooling properties. Among the various types of limestone available in India, Kota stone and Tandoor stone are the most widely used. These regional materials offer a durable, economical, and aesthetically pleasing flooring option, especially suited for the Indian climate.

In both heritage and modern architecture, these stones continue to play an important role—not just for their cost-efficiency, but for their timeless character. I have personally seen clients fall in love with the earthy texture and honest utility of these materials, especially when matched with a rustic, traditional, or minimalist design vision.

Types of Limestone

1. Kota Stone (Rajasthan)

- Available in blue, green, and brown shades.
- Non-porous with a smooth texture after polishing.

- Brown Kota, in particular, exhibits significant natural variation in shade and pattern from slab to slab. This inherent inconsistency gives it a rustic charm and that's its beauty.
- Available in both natural cleft and calibrated edge cut formats for easier laying and consistent thickness.
- Excellent for both interiors and exteriors.

2. **Tandoor Stone (Telangana & Karnataka)**
   - Comes in grey and bluish shades.
   - Slightly more porous than Kota.
   - Often used for verandas, courtyards, and pathways.

Comparison: Kota vs Tandoor

Feature	Kota Stone	Tandoor Stone
Stone Type	Limestone	Limestone
Color Variants	Blue, Green, Brown, Honey	Grey, Blue, Red
Surface Finish	Natural, Honed, Polished	Natural, Brushed, Shot-blasted
Texture	Smooth, fine-grained	Rough to slightly smooth
Water Absorption	Low	Moderate
Strength and Durability	High	High
Slip Resistance	Good	Very Good

Weather Resistance	Excellent (suitable for outdoors)	Good (can fade under strong sunlight)
Maintenance	Easy (periodic polishing)	Moderate (needs occasional sealing)
Applications	Flooring, pathways, corridors	Exterior paving, wall cladding, steps
Availability	Easily available in North India	Popular in South India (esp. Telangana)
Cost	Economical	Moderate
Aesthetic Appeal	Elegant and subtle	Rustic and traditional

Available Finishes

- **Natural Cleft:** Rough, rustic appearance
- **Polished:** Smooth, reflective finish (mostly seen in Kota)
- **Leather / Brushed:** Soft-textured, matte finish
- **Honed:** Satin-like smoothness with reduced gloss

General Applications

- Residential flooring (living, dining, bedrooms)
- Outdoor walkways, courtyards, verandas
- Institutional campuses and government buildings
- Rustic-style resorts, farmhouses, and cafes

Buying Guide

1. **Determine Application:** For indoor areas, prefer polished Kota. For outdoor spaces, natural or leather-finish Tandoor is ideal.
2. **Choose the Right Thickness:** 20–25 mm for interior use; 25–40 mm for exteriors or parking.
3. **Consider Finishing Options:** Kota Stone is now available in calibrated slabs (machine-cut to uniform thickness) and edge-cut varieties (sawn edges for straight alignment), which simplify installation and reduce wastage.
4. **Inspect for Cracks:** Always check slabs for hairline cracks or edges damage before purchase.
5. **Consistency:** Pick slabs with uniform shade and fewer patches or veins. Brown Kota, in particular, requires more careful selection due to its higher natural variation, however that high variation is part of its beauty and architects often choose it for themes that require a more organic, varied look.
6. **Moisture Test:** Pour water on the stone to see how quickly it's absorbed. Lower absorption = better durability.
7. **Measurement Clarification:** Although Kota slabs are typically cut to 22" x 22", pricing is often calculated assuming 24" x 24" coverage. Always confirm actual coverage and rates before purchase.
8. **Sourcing:** Purchase from a reliable quarry-based supplier to ensure quality and consistent thickness.

Installation Guide

1. **Substrate Preparation**
   a. Level the floor base using cement mortar.
   b. In outdoor areas, slope should be given for water drainage.
2. **Laying Procedure**
   a. Use cement mortar in a (1:4 ratio) for interior areas.
   b. For exteriors or moisture prone areas, use polymer modified mortar or tile adhesive for better bonding and flexibility.
   c. Leave 3–5 mm joints between slabs for grout filling and thermal expansion.
   d. Tap gently with a rubber mallet to ensure an even level and avoid air gaps.
3. **Joint Filling**
   a. Use cement-based grout for dry indoor areas.
   b. For outdoor spaces or wet zones, opt for epoxy grout to reduce seepage and stains.
4. **Curing**
   a. After laying, cure the floor with water sprinkling for 5–7 days.
   b. Prevent foot traffic during the curing phase to avoid disturbance or uneven setting.
5. **Surface Protection**
   a. Post installation, apply a high-quality penetrative stone sealer to enhance stain resistance and protect the natural texture.

b. Avoid acid-based cleaners as they can corrode or discolour limestone.

Tip: Reapply the stone sealer every 2–3 years to maintain longevity and colour vibrancy.

Final Thoughts

Limestone flooring, especially with Kota and Tandoor, is about embracing simplicity, strength, and timelessness. These natural stones have consistently proven their worth in the Indian climate, offering a cooling effect underfoot, elegant natural hues, and strong performance in both urban and rural settings.

Whether you're building a modern farmhouse, a traditional Haveli style home, or a contemporary outdoor patio—limestone is a material that will never go out of style. Its authenticity and enduring appeal make it a practical and aesthetic choice for generations to come.

CHAPTER 6

Terracotta and Clay Tiles

Rediscovering Tradition with Earthy Elegance

Terracotta and clay tiles are among the oldest forms of flooring and roofing materials used in Indian construction. Rich in heritage, sustainable in nature, and visually warm in tone, these tiles continue to find their place in modern architecture—bridging the gap between tradition and contemporary design.

As a strong advocate of materials that tell a story, I find terracotta tiles to be both timeless and soulful. They offer more than just a rustic aesthetic—they provide breathability, natural insulation, and a sense of grounded serenity that few other materials can match.

Types of Terracotta and Clay Tiles

1. **Handmade Terracotta Tiles**
    - Crafted using traditional methods.
    - Unique imperfections and color variations.
    - Suited for heritage-style or ethnic design.
2. **Machine-Made Clay Tiles**
    - Uniform in shape, size, and strength.

- More consistent in color.
- Suitable for contemporary, minimalist applications.

3. **Roofing Tiles**
    - Overlapping curved tiles designed for pitched roofs.
    - Available in Mangalore tiles, Spanish tiles, and flat roof profiles.
4. **Wall Cladding and Decorative Panels**
    - Hollow or carved clay blocks used for ventilated facades.
    - Lattice (jali) tiles for air flow and aesthetics.

Applications

- ➢ Flooring (indoors and verandas)
- ➢ Roofs for sloped structures
- ➢ Accent walls and façade cladding
- ➢ Pathways and garden landscaping
- ➢ Decorative murals, niches, and inlays

Available Sizes and Finishes

- ➢ **Floor Tiles:** 6"x6", 9"x9", 12"x12", Hexagonal, Brick Shapes
- ➢ **Wall Panels:** Louvered, embossed, Jali style
- ➢ **Finish Options:** Natural, wax polished, matte sealed, or glazed

> **Note:** Terracotta surfaces are typically porous and may darken with age or moisture exposure unless properly sealed.

Buying Guide

1. **Check for Porosity:** High porosity gives terracotta its breathability, but unsealed tiles can stain easily. Choose pre-sealed tiles or apply a sealant after installation for better protection.
2. **Surface Quality:** Inspect for cracks, warping, or excessive undulation especially in handmade tiles where irregularities are common.
3. **Consistency:** Machine-made tiles offer better dimensional accuracy; handmade ones have artisanal charm but need skilled laying for proper alignment.
4. **Colour Matching:** Order from a single batch or pre-sort to group similar tones for a more uniform appearance.
5. **Water Absorption Test:** Pour a few drops of water—good quality tiles will absorb slowly and dry evenly without blotching.
6. **Purpose-Based Selection:** Use anti-skid or textured finishes in wet zones or outdoor areas for safety and better grip.

Installation Guide

1. **Substrate and Surface Preparation**
   - **a.** Use a flat, stable cement base, free from dust and debris.
   - **b.** For heritage or restoration projects, lime mortar may be used for authenticity and breathability.
2. **Laying and Alignment**
   - **a.** Use a thin-set adhesive or semi-dry cement mortar (1:4 ratio) depending on the site conditions.

   b. Maintain 5–10 mm wide joints to accommodate natural expansion and contraction.
   c. Lay in running bond, brick, or diagonal patterns to enhance visual depth and rustic charm.
3. **Grouting**
   a. Use cement-based grout with mineral pigments to match or complement the tile tone.
   b. For higher durability, use epoxy grout in wet zones.
4. **Sealing**
   a. Apply a breathable penetrating sealer post-installation to protect against moisture absorption and staining.
   b. For indoor spaces, a natural wax or matte topcoat may be applied for added sheen and surface richness.
5. **Maintenance**
   a. Sweep or vacuum regularly.
   b. Mop with a pH neutral cleaner, non-acidic cleaner.
   c. Reseal every 2–3 years for lasting beauty.

Tip: Allow tiles to "breathe" by avoiding synthetic plastic coatings or laminates that block natural airflow and aging.

Final Thoughts

Terracotta and clay tiles bring warmth, authenticity, and tradition into the built environment. In a world of high-gloss finishes and artificial surfaces, these tiles offer a connection to the earth. Whether used in a modern villa or a heritage courtyard, terracotta always adds character, soul, and a sense of rooted elegance.

CHAPTER 7

Mosaic and Concrete Tiles

Craft Meets Utility in Modern Surfaces

Mosaic and concrete tiles are seeing a resurgence in popularity—not just for their design potential but also for their rugged durability and sustainable edge. From decorative inlays in *old havelis* to *trendy café floors* in urban cities, these tile types have proven adaptable, resilient, and creatively expressive.

Over the years, I've seen a renewed interest in mosaic and concrete tiles among architects looking for visual rhythm and character. They work wonderfully in both restoration projects and new age design, offering a perfect blend of tradition and innovation.

Types of Mosaic and Concrete Tiles

Terrazzo Tiles

- Made by embedding marble, granite, or glass chips into a cement base.
- Available in precast tile form or cast on site for seamless floors.

Installation Guide

1. **Base Preparation**
   a. Substrates must be clean, rigid, and level.
   b. Apply a layer of cement screed to provide cushioning and better bonding.
   c. Ensure surface moisture content is minimal before laying to avoid efflorescence.
2. **Adhesive & Laying**
   a. Use high bond tile adhesive (C2TE or C2TES1).
   b. For bigger tiles/slabs, go for a PU-based adhesive.
   c. Maintain 2–3 mm joints for cement tiles and 1–2 mm for terrazzo tiles.
3. **Grouting**
   a. Use white or grey cement grout.
   b. For terrazzo, epoxy grout may be used for durability and colour match. Ideally, go with the manufacturer's recommendation
4. **Surface Polishing**
   a. For on-site terrazzo, grinding and polishing is done after curing.
   b. Pre-polished tiles may need a final buff post-installation.
5. **Sealing and Maintenance**
   a. Apply a penetrating sealer for cement tiles.
   b. Avoid acidic cleaners, which damage the colour and finish.

Note: Mosaic and terrazzo tiles age gracefully and acquire a natural patina over time, which enhances their appeal.

- Timeless design, durable, and fully customizable in colour, size, and pattern.

Cement Concrete Tiles

- Also known as hydraulic tiles.
- Composed of pigmented cement and sand layers, mechanically pressed for strength.
- Popular for retro patterns and geometric designs.
- Increasingly used in facade cladding, especially in boutique buildings, villas, and cultural projects where visual identity is key.
- These tiles offer excellent thermal insulation, reduce heat gain, and can be fixed on vertical surfaces using mechanical systems or adhesives.
- Their matte, patterned finishes create surface texture and rhythm on exterior walls, making them ideal for contemporary architecture with a handcrafted feel.

Inlay Mosaic Tiles

- Feature artistic patterns using ceramic, glass, stone, or mother-of-pearl.
- Typically used for medallions, centerpieces, or custom wall murals.

Applications

- Entrance lobbies and living areas
- Stair risers and corridors
- Bathroom and kitchen accents
- Commercial restaurants and galleries
- Heritage and boutique properties

Design Styles Available

- **Classic Terrazzo:** Speckled surface in muted or bold tones
- **Victorian Patterns:** Geometric and floral designs
- **Retro Cement Patterns:** Monochrome or two-tone repeating tiles
- **Minimal Modern:** Fine-grained white terrazzo with soft pastel chips
- **Custom Inlays:** Borders, medallions, and Art Deco-inspired motifs

Buying Guide

1. **Tile Type:** Decide between terrazzo, concrete, or mosaic depending on visual and wear expectations.
2. **Size & Thickness:** Most tiles come in 8–12 mm thickness. For floors, choose 16–20 mm if high footfall is expected.
3. **Surface Polish:** Terrazzo is available in matte, honed, or mirror polished finishes.
4. **Slip Resistance:** Use matte or textured variants for wet zones.
5. **Check Edge Quality:** For uniform installation, inspect tiles for clean edges and dimensional accuracy.
6. **Pigment Stability:** Ensure the manufacturer uses UV stable pigments for outdoor or sun facing applications.
7. **Batch Consistency:** Always order from a single batch to avoid visual mismatches.

Final Thoughts

Concrete and mosaic tiles are not just utilitarian—they are artistic expressions that carry the legacy of traditional craft into modern settings. When installed thoughtfully and maintained well, they lend a bold identity to any space while ensuring strength and longevity.

CHAPTER 8

Marble Alternatives
Engineered Stone, Quartz & Composite Marble

The New Age Elegance in Surface Design

Natural marble is undeniably elegant—but it also comes with challenges such as high maintenance, porosity, and variation in shade and pattern. Fortunately, modern alternatives like engineered stone, quartz, and composite marble have emerged to offer the same luxurious appeal with added durability, consistency, and ease of use across applications.

In my experience, these alternatives provide an excellent solution for clients who want the beauty of marble without its unpredictability and upkeep concerns. Whether for countertops, floors, or cladding, engineered options are now a staple in both premium residential and commercial projects—delivering performance with precision.

Types of Marble Alternatives

1. **Engineered Quartz**
    - Made using 90–95% natural quartz crystals mixed with resin and pigments.

- Extremely hard and nonporous surface; does not absorb moisture or harbor bacteria.
- Available in a variety of solid colors and marble-like patterns with excellent surface uniformity.

2. **Composite Marble**
   - Made from marble dust and resin, molded into slabs or tiles under controlled conditions.
   - Mimics natural marble but with consistent color and fewer veins.
   - Lightweight and easier to cut and install than real marble, reducing installation time and wastage.
3. **Sintered Stone / Porcelain Slabs**
   - Made by compressing natural minerals under extremely high heat and pressure.
   - Ultracompact, UV resistant, stain proof, and scratch resistant—ideal for indoor and outdoor use.
   - Suitable for countertops, facades, and high-end furniture tops, and even for floors.

Applications

- Kitchen countertops and backsplashes
- Bathroom vanities and wall cladding
- Flooring in luxury apartments or offices
- Elevator lobby walls and reception areas
- Table tops and bar counters
- Staircase
- Window sills and door frames

Advantages Over Natural Marble

- **Nonporous:** No sealing required; resists stains and moisture.
- **Stain & Scratch Resistant:** Ideal for high-use zones like kitchens and bathrooms.
- **Consistency:** Uniform color and pattern throughout.
- **Easy to Install:** Lighter weight and consistent thickness make handling easier.
- **Eco-friendly:** Many brands use recycled content or energy-efficient production methods.

Buying Guide

1. **Application Purpose:** Choose Engineered Quartz or Sintered Stone for high-use kitchens, Composite Marble for decorative interiors, and sintered stone for outdoor or high-performance areas.
2. **Finish Options:** Available in matte, satin, polished, and textured surfaces—each suited to different design needs and functional uses.
3. **Thickness:** Standard slabs are available in 15 mm and 20 mm variants. Choose based on application load and design preference.
4. **Edge Profiles:** Engineered stone allows for clean-cut edges and various profiles (bevelled, ogee, bullnose).
5. **Brand Reputation:** Stick with established brands for quality assurance, warranty, and stain resistance certification.

6. **Colour Matching:** Always inspect slabs physically before fabrication to check for batch tone consistency—especially important for large or visible surfaces.

Installation Guide

1. **Surface Preparation**
    a. Ensure level and stable platform (especially for countertops).
    b. Use moisture resistant base boards for bathroom and kitchen installations.
2. **Cutting and Handling**
    a. Use water-cooled machines with diamond blades.
    b. Avoid dry cuts to prevent chipping or resin burns.
    c. Cutting these slabs requires proper skill and training. Since this product is relatively new in Indian markets, many tile installers may not be fully aware of correct methods. Refer to manufacturers training guides or videos for the best results.
3. **Adhesive Application**
    a. Use polymer modified or epoxy-based adhesives.
    b. Apply uniformly with a notched trowel; allow for necessary expansion joints.
4. **Joint Treatment**
    a. Minimize visible joints using color-matched adhesives.
    b. Fill gaps with non-shrinking resin-based filler.
5. **Cleaning & Protection**
    a. Clean with pH neutral cleaners.

b. Avoid bleach or acidic chemicals.

c. Cover installed surfaces during ongoing work to avoid scratches.

Tip: Always follow the slab manufacturer's recommended adhesive and fabrication guidelines to ensure proper performance and maintain warranty coverage.

Final Thoughts

Marble alternatives like quartz, composite marble, and sintered stone are redefining luxury surfaces. They bring together the best of both worlds—sophisticated looks and high functionality. With continued technological advancements, these materials are no longer just alternatives—they represent a smart, future-ready choice for modern spaces.

CHAPTER 9

Wooden Flooring
Solid, Engineered & Laminates

Warmth, Character, and Timeless Appeal

Wooden flooring continues to captivate homeowners and designers alike for its natural warmth, tactile beauty, and the classic ambience it creates in a space. While natural wood has been used for centuries, new technologies have brought forward engineered wood and laminate flooring options that combine aesthetics with enhanced durability and affordability.

Having worked closely with premium flooring solutions for years, I find that wood-look floors—whether natural or synthetic—bring an unmatched richness and coziness to residential interiors, hospitality projects, and even boutique commercial spaces.

Types of Wooden Flooring

1. Solid Hardwood Flooring

- Made from a single piece of natural wood.
- Available in species like oak, teak, walnut, maple, and ash.
- Offers longevity and the ability to be sanded and refinished multiple times.

2. Engineered Wood Flooring

- Constructed with a top hardwood veneer over plywood or HDF (High-Density Fiberboard) base.
- Provides the look of solid wood with greater dimensional stability.
- Suitable for places with moderate humidity or underfloor heating systems.

3. Laminate Flooring

- Multi-layered synthetic flooring with a photographic wood-look surface.
- Economical, scratch-resistant, and easy to install with click-lock systems.
- Not suitable for wet areas or zones with high moisture exposure.

Applications

- Living rooms, bedrooms, and dining spaces
- Hospitality suites and boutique retail stores
- Engineered wood is suitable for moderate-use kitchens and low-moisture zones
- Laminate flooring is ideal for fast makeovers and rental properties

> **Note:** Avoid using wooden flooring in bathrooms, outdoor areas, or high-humidity zones unless specifically treated for moisture resistance.

Finishes and Sizes

- **Finishes:** Matte, semi-gloss, high-gloss, hand-scraped, brushed, stained, smoked
- **Edge Profiles:** Square edge, bevelled edge, micro bevel
- **Sizes:**
  - Planks range from 120 mm to 250 mm wide
  - Lengths vary between 600 mm and 2400 mm
  - Thickness: 8 mm (laminate), 12–15 mm (engineered), 18–22 mm (solid wood)

Buying Guide

1. **Usage Area:** Choose engineered wood for long-term durability in climate variable zones; use laminate for budget-friendly and quick installations.
2. **Wear Rating – AC Classification:**
   a. **AC1:** Light residential use (bedrooms, low-traffic zones)
   b. **AC2:** General residential (living rooms, dining areas)
   c. **AC3:** Heavy residential/light commercial (hallways, offices)
   d. **AC4:** General commercial use (retail stores, showrooms)
   e. **AC5:** Heavy commercial traffic (malls, public spaces)
   f. Laminate flooring is usually classified from AC1 to AC5 based on abrasion resistance; higher the rating, greater the durability.
   g. Engineered wood doesn't follow AC ratings. Instead,

it is measured by veneer thickness and core stability; thicker top layers (3–6 mm) offer better durability and re-sanding capability.

3. **Wood Species:** Hardwoods like oak and teak are more durable than softer woods like pine or birch.
4. **Finish:** Go for matte or textured finishes in high-traffic zones to reduce visible wear.
5. **Underlay & Acoustic Backing:** Use noise reducing foam underlays in apartments or multi-storey homes.
6. **Scratch and Water Resistance:** Laminate offers better surface scratch resistance; engineered wood handles humidity better than solid wood.
7. **Brand and Warranty:** Reputed brands offer better locking systems and longer warranties.
8. **Sustainability:** Look for FSC-certified or recycled wood-based flooring options.

Installation Guide

1. **Subfloor Preparation**
   a. Ensure the subfloor is level, clean, and moisture free.
   b. Use a moisture barrier sheet, especially for ground floor or basement applications.
2. **Installation Methods**
   a. **Solid Wood:** Nail down or glue down installation on wooden subfloors.
   b. **Engineered Wood:** Can be glued down or installed as a floating floor.

   c. **Laminate:** Click-lock floating floor system is most common and DIY-friendly.

3. **Expansion Gaps**
   a. Leave a 10–12 mm expansion gap around the perimeter to account for natural expansion and contraction due to temperature and humidity changes.
4. **Finishing Touches**
   a. Use skirting boards, transition trims, and end caps for a clean look.
   b. Allow acclimatization of wooden planks for 48–72 hours before installation to avoid warping.

Tip: Never mop wooden flooring with excess water. Use a damp microfiber cloth for cleaning.

Final Thoughts

Wooden flooring adds a soulful character that synthetic materials rarely achieve. With modern engineered and laminate options, it's possible to enjoy the aesthetic charm of wood in a variety of budgets and applications. Proper installation, routine maintenance, and choosing the right type for your environment are key to long-lasting performance.

CHAPTER 10

Vinyl and SPC Flooring
Versatility Meets Practicality

Vinyl and SPC (Stone Polymer Composite) flooring have emerged as high-performance alternatives for modern homes and commercial spaces. These materials are known for their water resistance, easy installation, and impressive variety of designs—including wood, stone, cement, and abstract prints.

In recent years, I've seen a rapid shift toward these materials, especially in renovation projects and budget-sensitive builds. They are not only quick to install but also offer long-lasting results with minimal maintenance.

Types of Vinyl & SPC Flooring

1. **Vinyl Plank Flooring (LVT)**
    - Mimics wood or tile in long plank form.
    - Flexible yet durable.
    - Ideal for bedrooms, living rooms, and dry zones.
2. **Sheet Vinyl**
    - Rolled material laid out in large, seamless sheets.
    - Best suited for budget projects and large floor areas.

3. SPC Flooring (Stone Polymer Composite)

- SPC stands for Stone Polymer Composite or Stone Plastic Composite.
- It consists of multiple layers:
  - UV Coating for scratch and stain resistance
  - Wear Layer that protects against abrasion
  - Decor Film that replicates the look of wood, stone, or other finishes
  - SPC Core made from limestone powder, PVC, and stabilizers for rigidity and water resistance
  - Underlayment (optional) for cushioning and acoustic insulation
- Offers higher dimensional stability and impact resistance compared to traditional vinyl.
- Best suited for kitchens, bathrooms, basements, and semi-commercial areas.

Applications

- ➢ Residential bedrooms and living areas
- ➢ Rental apartments and quick renovation projects
- ➢ Offices, salons, cafes, and retail stores
- ➢ Wet areas like kitchens and powder rooms (especially SPC)

Key Features

- ➢ 100% water-resistant (SPC)
- ➢ UV protected top layer for colour stability
- ➢ Acoustic insulation with inbuilt underlayment (in select models)

- Click-lock or glue down installation systems
- Variety of designs including wood grain, stone, and terrazzo patterns

Buying Guide

1. **Choose Between Vinyl and SPC:** Use vinyl planks for low-footfall dry zones; choose SPC for wet areas or heavy use.
2. **Core Composition:** SPC offers more strength due to its stone polymer core.
3. **Wear Layer Thickness:**
    a. **0.2 mm:** Light residential
    b. **0.3 mm:** Standard residential and light commercial
    c. **0.5 mm+:** Heavy commercial
4. **Surface Texture:** Embossed or hand-scraped finishes add realism.
5. **Click vs. Glue:** Click-lock systems are DIY friendly; glue down is better for large commercial floors.
6. **Underlayment:** Select SPC with integrated underlayment for sound insulation and added comfort.
7. **Certifications:** Look for floors with GreenGuard, FloorScore, or ISO certifications for indoor air safety.

Installation Guide

1. **Subfloor Preparation**
    a. Ensure the subfloor is flat, dry, and clean.
    b. Minor undulations can be corrected using a levelling compound.

2. **Acclimatization**
    a. Allow flooring to acclimate to room temperature for 24–48 hours.
3. **Laying Method**
    a. Use the click-lock system for DIY or floating floors.
    b. The glue down method requires adhesive to be spread evenly with a trowel.
4. **Expansion Gaps**
    a. Leave 5–8 mm expansion gaps around walls and doorways.
5. **Finishing**
    a. Install skirting and transition profiles for neat finish.
    b. Avoid wet mopping for 72 hours post-installation.

Maintenance

- Sweep or vacuum regularly.
- Mop using pH-neutral vinyl floor cleaner.
- Avoid dragging heavy furniture without felt pads.
- Refrain from using abrasive scrubbers or strong solvents.

SPC floors are ideal for homes with pets and children due to their scratch and moisture resistance.

Final Thoughts

Vinyl and SPC flooring have redefined affordable flooring without compromising on design. Their versatility, quick installation, and resistance to daily wear make them a go-to option for modern homes and commercial spaces alike.

Part 3

From Showroom to Site

How to Avoid Regret

CHAPTER 11

The Ultimate Flooring Checklist You Must Have

Your Step-by-step Guide Before Making the Purchase

When it comes to flooring and wall surfaces, informed decision making is crucial—not just to match aesthetics but also to ensure performance and longevity. Whether you're a homeowner building from scratch or renovating an existing space, a solid checklist can help avoid costly mistakes, wastage, and regrets.

With decades of experience guiding customers, I've prepared a smart checklist that simplifies your selection, budgeting, and coordination process.

- **Pre Planning Essentials**
  - Identify Application Area
  - Indoor vs. Outdoor
  - Wall vs. Floor
  - Wet vs. Dry Zone
- **Set Budget Ranges**
  - Establish per sq. ft. rate (product + laying)
  - Include buffer for wastage and sealing/coating costs

- **Understand Your Aesthetic Preferences**
  - Natural, earthy, rustic, luxurious, modern?
  - Do you prefer a uniform tone or natural variation?
- **Measure Accurately**
  - Note total floor area + vertical wall areas (bathrooms/ kitchens)
  - Include skirting, staircase risers, balcony edges
  - Add 5–10% for cutting wastage and breakage

Showroom Visit Tips

1. Carry Site Layouts or Floor Plans
2. Click Photos of the Current Space (if renovating)
3. Take Reference Images or Moodboards
4. Ask for Sample Tiles or Slabs for Onsite Comparison
5. Check Real-Life Mock-ups or Displays
6. Review Available Stock vs. Lead Time

Technical Verifications

1. Check Tile Grade or Stone Hardness (especially for high-traffic areas)
2. Water Absorption Rate (important for outdoor and wet areas)
3. Surface Finish Grip (for anti-slip requirements)
4. Adhesive & Laying Recommendation by supplier or technician
5. Ensure Batch Consistency & Shade Matching

Coordination with Contractors

1. Discuss Joint Widths and Grouting Preferences
2. Confirm Expansion Gaps for Wood/Vinyl/SPC

3. Schedule Material Delivery Ahead of Time
4. Inspect Before Installation
5. Oversee the First Few Rows Laid to Confirm Pattern and Alignment

Tip: Maintain a written list of selected materials, tile codes, finish details, and quantities to cross-check during unloading and laying.

Final Thoughts

A good flooring or cladding decision doesn't just depend on choosing the right material—it's also about preparation, measurement, and execution. This checklist ensures that you go from showroom to site with confidence, clarity, and complete control.

CHAPTER 12

What No One Tells You

Adhesives, Grout & Joints That Actually Matter

Moving Beyond Sand and Cement

Traditional tile laying methods relied heavily on sand-cement mortar, but modern construction demands speed, precision, hygiene, and longevity. Enter tile adhesives and epoxy grouts—game-changing innovations that have transformed the way we install floor and wall tiles.

Having observed hundreds of residential and commercial sites, I can confidently say that the difference between a *good finish* and a *great one* often lies in the choice of adhesive and grout. In this chapter, we'll understand why these materials matter and how they solve problems that conventional methods simply cannot.

Why Shift from Cement Mortar to Tile Adhesives?

Parameter	Tile Adhesive	Cement Mortar

Surface Preparation	Minimal priming required	Requires soaking and curing
Mixing Consistency	Pre-mixed; uniform quality	Manual mixing, inconsistent
Bond Strength	High (meets EN 12004 standards)	Moderate; can delaminate
Tile Types Supported	Suitable for all tile types including vitrified & large-format	Mainly for basic ceramic tiles
Application Thickness	3–6 mm (thin-bed application)	10–25 mm (thick-bed application)
Load on Structure	Low dead load	Heavy dead load
Setting Time	Fast setting; ready for use in 24 hrs	Slow setting; 3–7 days required
Water Absorption Dependency	Works with low-absorption tiles	Needs high-absorption tiles
Vertical Installation (Walls)	Excellent adhesion; no slippage	May need support; tile slippage common
Wastage	Minimal material wastage	High wastage during mixing and application
Grouting Time	Ready for grouting in 24 hrs	Delayed grouting (3–4 days)

Suitability for Wet Areas	High water resistance	Low water resistance
Compliance with Standards	Conforms to EN 12004 (C1/C2/S1/S2 grades)	No defined performance standard
Labor Efficiency	Easy & fast application	Time-consuming; needs highly skilled labor
Cost Efficiency (Long-term)	Low maintenance; fewer repairs	High maintenance; rework common

Note: In tiled walls and vertical installations, traditional cement mortar often fails to achieve proper curing and bonding. Tile adhesives overcome this by eliminating the need for prolonged water curing—ensuring better grip, faster turnaround, and longer-lasting results.

Role of Tile Adhesives in Modern Installations

1. **Premixed & Consistent:** Eliminates site mixing errors and ensures uniform performance.
2. **Thin bed Application:** Saves flooring height and avoids unnecessary weight on the structure.
3. **No Curing Required:** Ideal for wall tiles, large-format tiles, and vitrified tiles where water-based curing is impractical.
4. **Adhesive Grades Available:**

   C1: For ceramic tiles on interior walls/floors

   C2T: For vitrified, porcelain, or large-format tiles

C2TE: For vertical surfaces and outdoor surfaces

C2TES1/S2: For high-traffic, submerged areas, or applications requiring flexibility and deformability

Importance of Spacer Joints

Spacer joints are no longer optional—they are essential for:

- **Even Grouting:** Helps maintain uniform width for aesthetic and functional grout lines
- **Thermal Expansion:** Prevents tile cracking and buckling under heat or movement
- **Precision & Alignment:** Ensures symmetrical layout and clean finish

Recommended joint widths:

Generally, as per Design and Individual Preference

- 1–3 mm for vitrified and porcelain tiles
- 3–5 mm for ceramic and natural stone tiles
- 4–10 mm for exterior installations or rustic tiles

Grout Filling: Cement vs. Epoxy Grouts

Feature	Cement Grout	Epoxy Grout
Material Composition	Cement-based with sand and additives	Epoxy resin, hardener, and filler powder
Water Resistance	Moderate (can absorb moisture)	Excellent (non-porous)

Stain Resistance	Low (prone to staining)	High (very stain resistant)
Chemical Resistance	Low	High
Durability	Moderate (may crack over time)	Very high (resistant to cracks)
Flexibility	Low	High
Color Retention	Fades over time	Excellent, does not fade
Shrinkage/ Cracking	High (can crack with movement)	Low (flexible and crack-resistant)
Ease of Cleaning	Difficult to clean when stained	Easy to clean even after long time
Installation Complexity	Easy to apply, especially for beginners	Requires skilled application
Cost	Low	High
Curing Time	24 to 72 hours	4 to 24 hours
Recommended Areas	Residential floors, low-moisture areas	Kitchens, bathrooms, industrial & wet areas

Note: Epoxy grouts are especially recommended for bathrooms, kitchens, and commercial spaces where hygiene and durability are essential.

Installation Tips

1. Always use notched trowels for even adhesive spread
2. Back butter large format tiles to ensure full bonding
3. Use spacers and levelling clips to maintain proper alignment
4. Clean adhesive and grout overflow before it hardens
5. Protect tiled areas from water and load for at least 24–48 hours

Final Thoughts

Modern adhesives and grouts are no longer just accessories—they are core components of a successful installation. They ensure better bonding, save time, reduce maintenance, and significantly improve the life and look of tiled surfaces.

Switching from traditional methods to adhesive-based installation is not a trend—it's a necessity for precision, performance, and peace of mind.

CHAPTER 13

How to Avoid Costly Flooring Mistakes

Do's & Don'ts That Actually Matter

Build it Right the First Time

Flooring and cladding are big-ticket investments—not just in money, but also in looks, durability, and first impressions. And yet, it's often the small things—a wrong tile choice, poor handling, or missed detail during installation—that snowball into major, costly problems.

After spending nearly three decades in the industry, I've seen where most people go wrong... and how simple it is to get it right with a few sharp checks in place. This chapter brings you the do's and don'ts that actually matter—the practical wisdom that's not found in manuals, but learned through real mistakes and real experience.

If you're building or renovating, consider this your flooring mistake-prevention guide—whether you're the homeowner, architect, or the one in charge at the site.

Do's: Best Practices

☑ Planning & Design

- Do measure accurately and plan for tile layout in advance.
- Do consider future expansion joints, plumbing slopes, and transitions.
- Do consult material experts when selecting for wet zones, exteriors, or driveways.
- Do factor in strength, slip resistance, and surface finish early during the design stage based on usage area.

☑ Material Handling

- Do inspect material upon delivery for cracks, chips, or color mismatch.
- Do store tiles or slabs on flat and dry surfaces.
- Do mix tiles from multiple boxes to even out natural variation.
- Do check edge finish and size uniformity before installation to ensure a perfect fit.

☑ Installation

- Do use adhesives instead of cement mortar, especially for vitrified tiles and vertical surfaces.
- Do use spacers and leveling clips to ensure even joints and neat finish.
- Do allow curing or bonding time as recommended by the manufacturer.
- Do pre-check for slip rating and surface grip—especially in

wet or sloped areas.

☑ **Finishing**

- Do apply a stone sealer for porous stones like sandstone, limestone, and marble.
- Do clean excess grout immediately after filling.
- Do use epoxy grout in kitchens, bathrooms, and commercial zones.

☑ **Maintenance**

- Do use pH neutral cleaners for natural stones and tile surfaces.
- Do reseal natural stone floors every 2–3 years for protection.

Don'ts: Common Pitfalls to Avoid

✕ **Material Selection**

- Don't choose high gloss tiles for bathroom floors—they are slippery.
- Don't use ceramic wall tiles on floors—they lack surface strength.
- Don't ignore slip resistance or load-bearing strength based on area usage.

✕ **Installation Errors**

- Don't skip substrate levelling and curing - it leads to tile lippage.
- Don't lay tiles edge to edge without spacers - they will crack under stress.
- Don't delay grouting beyond 24 hours of tile laying.

✕ **Site Mismanagement**

- ➢ Don't drag heavy furniture without felt pads or protection.
- ➢ Don't use acid cleaners—they erode natural surfaces and grouts.
- ➢ Don't walk over freshly laid tiles for at least 24–48 hours.
- ➢ Don't neglect final checks for smoothness, color match, and finish—this is the last mile of quality control.

Bonus Tips

- ➢ Always keep 10% extra material for future repairs or patchwork.
- ➢ Photograph layouts or tile arrangements for reference before final grouting.
- ➢ Educate your site team on tile names, laying pattern, and adhesive type.

> **Tip:** A few minutes of planning and checklist review can prevent hours of rectification later.

Final Thoughts

Flooring and cladding are high investment decisions—not just financially, but visually and structurally. Following these do's and don'ts ensures that your project looks beautiful and lasts long, with minimal upkeep and zero regrets.

Part 4

Care, Cost & Lifetime Value

CHAPTER 14

How to Make Your Floors Last 20+ Years with Simple Maintenance Tips

Protect Your Investment with the Right Care

Your floors go through a lot—daily foot traffic, spills, furniture movement, and regular cleaning. If you want them to stay beautiful, strong, and hygienic for the next 20+ years, the secret lies in simple, consistent maintenance.

This chapter shows you exactly how to maintain every type of flooring and cladding—from ceramic tiles and natural stones to wood, vinyl, and more. With the right approach, you won't just clean your floors... you'll preserve them. Let's dive into the most practical, easy-to-follow tips that will keep your surfaces looking new for decades.

General Maintenance Tips for All Surfaces

- Sweep or vacuum regularly to remove dust and debris.
- Use pH-neutral cleaners—avoid acidic, bleach-based, or abrasive products.

- ➢ Wipe spills immediately to prevent stains or surface etching.
- ➢ Use doormats at entrances to reduce dirt and grit.
- ➢ Avoid dragging furniture—use felt pads or lift instead.
- ➢ Rotate rugs periodically to prevent uneven fading.
- ➢ Ensure good ventilation in wet areas to avoid mold or moisture build-up.

Material Wise Cleaning Guidelines

☑ **Ceramic & Vitrified Tiles**

- Mop with warm water and mild liquid detergent.
- Use grout safe brushes to clean joints.
- Regrout or touch up joints every few years for hygiene and aesthetics.

☑ **Natural Stones (Marble, Granite, Kota, Sandstone)**

- Use stone safe cleaners only—never use acid or vinegar.
- Reseal every 2–3 years depending on footfall and finish.
- Polish or buff periodically to maintain gloss and remove light scratches .

☑ **Engineered & Laminate Wood Flooring**

- Clean with a damp microfiber cloth.
- Avoid excess water, wet mopping, or steam cleaners.
- Use wood-safe floor cleaners with no wax or polish.

☑ **Terracotta and Cement Tiles**

- Clean with soft brush and gentle soap.
- Apply penetrating sealer every 2–3 years.
- Avoid constant moisture exposure—dry thoroughly.

☑ SPC & Vinyl Flooring

- Mop with a vinyl safe cleaner; avoid soaking the floor.
- Avoid harsh scrubbing pads or solvent cleaners.
- Check for joint openings periodically and fix promptly.

☑ Grout & Joint Care

- For cement grout, avoid excessive water and reseal yearly if needed.
- For epoxy grout, scrub gently with mild soap and soft non-abrasive pad.
- Replace cracked or deteriorated joints before water seeps underneath.

Periodic Maintenance Schedule

Frequency	Task
Daily / Weekly	Sweeping, Dry Mopping, Spill Cleaning, Spill Cleanup
Monthly	Wet Mopping (always use Clean Dirt Free Water), Grout and Joint Inspection
Yearly	Resealing (Stones, Terracotta, Marble, Terrazzo)
2 – 3 years	Deep Clean + Reseal + Repolish (Marble and Terrazzo) + Minor Repairs

Tip: Maintain a flooring care log—especially for large projects or commercial spaces—to schedule regular upkeep.

Final Thoughts

With a small amount of regular care and attention, your floors and walls can remain stunning for decades. The materials you choose are strong, but their longevity depends on how you treat them post-installation. Maintenance is not a chore—it's a commitment to preserving beauty, hygiene, and value.

Your Journey Doesn't End Here

Thank you for your valuable time and for being part of this journey.

You've just explored what feels like a complete Wikipedia of how to choose the right flooring, wall surfaces, and modern materials—built from years of on-site experience, real problems, and practical solutions.

Now, you have two choices:

You can use this book as your map and walk the path on your own—everything you need is here.

Or

If you'd prefer me to walk alongside you—whether it's to clear a doubt, help with a selection, or just talk through your plan—I'm just one message away.

Feel free to book a 1-to-1 meeting or reach out for any queries related to this book.

Email me at: abhishek.avmgranite@gmail.com

Let's build it right, together.

With Warm Regards,
Abhishek Malani

Glossary

- **AC Rating:** Abrasion Class rating, indicating the wear resistance of laminate flooring.
- **Adhesive Grades (C1, C2T, C2TE, etc.):** Classification indicating the strength and flexibility of tile adhesives.
- **Back-Buttering:** Technique of applying adhesive to the back of tiles to ensure better adhesion.
- **Bevelled Edge:** A sloped edge finish on wooden or laminate planks that creates a visible groove between boards.
- **Composite Marble:** Artificial marble made from marble dust combined with resin.
- **Cladding:** Covering an exterior or interior wall with stone, tile, wood, or synthetic material for aesthetic and protective purposes.
- **Cement Grout:** A mix of cement and additives used to fill tile joints. Affordable but less stain-resistant than epoxy grout.
- **Engineered Wood:** Flooring made from layers of wood veneers glued together.
- **Epoxy Grout:** Resin-based grout known for high strength, waterproofing, and stain resistance.

- **Expansion Joint:** A deliberate gap left between materials (tiles/wood) to accommodate expansion and contraction due to temperature or humidity.
- **GVT (Glazed Vitrified Tiles):** Tiles coated with a glazed layer, offering design versatility and durability.
- **Joint Spacer:** A plastic or rubber insert used during tile installation to maintain uniform gaps between tiles.
- **Laminate Flooring:** A synthetic floorboard with a photographic layer mimicking wood or stone, usually installed with a click-lock system.
- **Leveling Clips:** Tools used during tile laying to ensure all tiles are level and flush, especially with large format tiles.
- **Lippage:** A height difference between two adjacent tiles, usually due to uneven installation.
- **PEI Rating (Porcelain Enamel Institute):** Indicates abrasion resistance of ceramic tiles.
- **PGVT (Polished Glazed Vitrified Tiles):** Glazed vitrified tiles polished for a glossy finish.
- **R-Value:** Indicates slip resistance of flooring materials.
- **SPC (Stone Plastic Composite):** A durable flooring type made from limestone powder, PVC, and stabilizers.
- **Sintered Stone/SPC:** Advanced materials created under high pressure and temperature for ultra durability and water resistance.
- **Subfloor:** The base layer beneath the final floor finish, usually made of concrete or wood, which must be clean and level before laying.

- **Spacer Joints:** Gaps deliberately left between tiles to allow for expansion and even grout application.
- **Underlayment:** A thin layer placed between the subfloor and flooring for insulation, cushioning, or soundproofing.
- **Veneer (Wood):** A thin slice of natural wood used as the top layer in engineered wood flooring.
- **Vitrified Tiles:** Non-porous tiles made by firing at very high temperatures, known for their strength and water resistance.